220.9'505

Ross, Bill   8876 HC

ROS

(JR)

Hey, that's not what the Bible
says, too!

8876 HC

220.9'505

Ross, Bill

ROS

(JR)

Hey, that's not what the Bible
says too!

SEP 0 1 2003
9.99

Written and Illustrated by
Bill Ross

Thomas Nelson, Inc.
Nashville

Copyright © 2000 by Bill Ross

Published in Nashville, Tennessee, by Tommy Nelson®, a division of Thomas Nelson, Inc.

Bible stories are based on the *International Children's Bible*, New Century Version, copyright © 1986, 1988, 1999 by Tommy Nelson®, a division of Thomas Nelson, Inc.

Scripture quotations used in this book are from the *Holy Bible*, New King James Version (NKJV), copyright © 1979, 1980, 1982 by Thomas Nelson, Inc., Publisher.

Library of Congress Cataloging-in-Publication Data
Ross, Bill, 1956-
    Hey, that's not what the Bible says too! / written and illustrated by Bill Ross.
       p. cm.
   ISBN 0-8499-7592-1
   1. Bible stories, English. 2. Bible–Juvenile humor. [1. Bible stories.] I. Title: Hey, that is not what the Bible says too!. II. Title.
BS551.2.R58 2000
220.9'505–dc21   00-048946

Printed in the United States of America

00 01 02 03 04 QWT 9 8 7 6 5 4 3 2 1

For my really (enter mushy, loving adjective here)
wife, Barb.

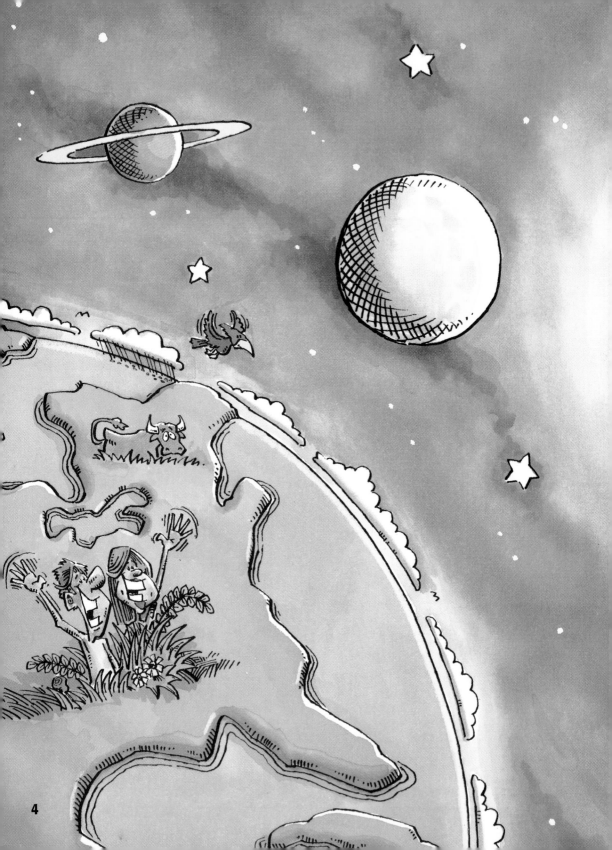

In the very beginning, before there was anything, God created everything. I'm talking about EVERYTHING. Oceans, dirt, and planets. Cows, stars, and pineapples. People, ponds, and bugs. Everything. He worked very hard, and it took Him six days to make all this stuff.

But God's work wasn't finished. He spent
the seventh day cleaning up the mess He
made while He was creating everything.

8

Actually, on the seventh day, God rested and said that day was holy. We praise God every day, but we set aside a day of rest each week to worship and praise God with others.

Turn to page 66 to read the real, true story of Creation from the Book of Genesis.

God made a promise
to old man Abraham
and his old wife Sarah.
They didn't have any
children, but God promised
them that they would have
a son. Sarah found this
very hard to believe.

Sure enough, the next
day, the stork came to
their door with a beautiful,
bouncing, baby boy!

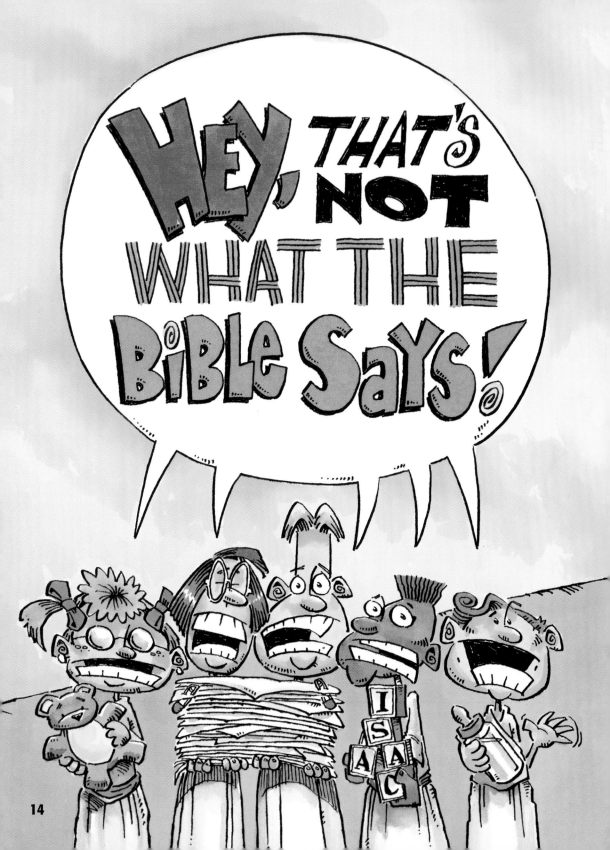

No, the stork doesn't bring babies.
Sarah had her baby boy God's
way. His name was Isaac, and
he became the father of many
nations. God **ALWAYS** keeps
His promises.

Turn to page 67 to read the real,
true *story of Abraham and Sarah
from the Book of Genesis.*

Jacob had twelve sons. But he wanted to give a special gift to his youngest son, Joseph, who was special to Jacob.

He **THOUGHT** and he **THOUGHT.**

Jacob gave Joseph a brand-new pair of expensive pump, Velcro, grid, max basketball shoes! Joseph loved those new shoes. His brothers thought he was SOOO COOL.

With those new shoes on his feet, he could run faster and jump higher than any shepherd around.

Jacob gave his favorite son Joseph a new coat of many colors. His brothers were very jealous—they wanted new coats too. They were so angry that they did mean things to Joseph, but God took care of Joseph. Because of God's love, Joseph forgave his brothers.

Turn to page 68 to read the real, true story of Joseph and His Brothers from the Book of Genesis.

God's people were slaves in Egypt. Then God had them set free.

God promised them a land of their own. As they were on their long journey to the Promised Land, they became very hungry and very upset. "When we were slaves in Egypt, at least we had a bunch of food. Now we're going to starve to death.

"WHAT KIND OF DEAL IS THIS?"

Luckily, over the very next hill, they came to a fast-food
restaurant that had camel burgers and Pharaoh fries.
The kids all got JOYFUL MEALS with little plastic
plague toys.

25

In the morning, the people found that God had made it rain yummy-tasting bread. They called the stuff **MANNA**, which means "what is it?" Each family gathered as much as they needed for the day. This is how God provided for their needs.

Turn to page 69 to read the real, true story of Manna in the Desert from the Book of Exodus.

God had some special thoughts he wanted to tell Moses about how we should live our lives. God wanted Moses to share them with the rest of the people.

God told Moses to go to a mountaintop.

29

On the mountaintop, Moses found a jar where God had placed **TEN PRETTY GOOD IDEAS**. He asked Moses to pick a couple of them. He picked "Share your toys if you feel like it" and "Always save room for your dessert."

Moses received the Ten Commandments from God—ten very important rules God wants people to live by. Just like in a game, we need to know the rules so we'll do the right thing and not do the wrong thing.

Turn to page 70 to read the real, true story of the Ten Commandments from the Book of Exodus.

1. Don't believe in other gods.
2. Don't love anything more than God.
3. Don't use God's name in a bad way.
4. Keep church-day Holy.
5. Love your Mother and Father.
6. Do not kill.
7. Be faithful to your spouse.
8. Do not steal.
9. Do not tell lies.
10. Don't want what other people have.

God told Gideon that He would help him defeat the enemies of his people. Gideon was nervous and afraid, and he wasn't sure that he heard God correctly.

How could he be sure what God said was true?

He asked a referee to help him. Gideon told him to flip a coin.
"**HEADS** . . . God helps me. **TAILS** . . . He won't."

Gideon did something unusual to make sure God was with him. Gideon laid a piece of cloth on the ground before he went to bed.

He asked God to make the cloth wet and the ground around it dry. This would prove to Gideon that God would help him. And that is what God did.

To be **REALLY** sure, the next night Gideon asked God to make the *ground* wet and keep the material dry. And that is what God did. Gideon now knew God would be with him in the battle, just as He had said He would.

Turn to page 73 to read the real, true story of Gideon from the Book of Judges.

God chose a special young woman named Mary, who was to be married to Joseph, to have a baby boy who would grow up to be the Savior of the world.

This baby named Jesus was God's Son. Mary knew Jesus was a pretty **SPECIAL** kid.

So she hired a big-shot agent, held a **HUGE PRESS CONFERENCE**, and told the world of the newborn King of God's people.

Mary and Joseph actually had to keep quiet about baby Jesus. King Herod, the ruler of the land, was jealous of Jesus and wanted the baby killed. One night an angel appeared to Joseph in his dream to tell him to take his new family to Egypt. They would be safe there until Herod died.

Turn to page 74 to read the real, true *story of Mary and Baby Jesus from the Book of Matthew.*

Years later, when He was twelve, Jesus, along with Joseph and Mary, went to Jerusalem for a celebration.

On their way home, after traveling all day, Joseph and Mary were alarmed to discover that Jesus was not with them. They went back to Jerusalem and looked for Jesus for three days.

They found Jesus at the mall playing **VIDEO GAMES,** where He'd been playing one game for three days on a single shekel.

They finally found Jesus in the Temple with the wise religious leaders, learning about God. Everyone was amazed at how such a young boy could be so wise about the things of God.

Turn to page 77 to read the real, true story of Young Jesus in the Temple from the Book of Luke.

After three years of teaching and performing miracles, Jesus brought His disciples together for a final time before He had to leave them.

He had something **VERY IMPORTANT** to share with them.

The disciples were thrilled when Coach Jesus handed out
new soccer uniforms to everyone.

He wanted **THE DISCIPLE DOMINATORS** to look like champs for their first season in the NTSL (New Testament Soccer League).

It was a very serious time together. Jesus shared bread and wine, and He talked of His death, which would soon happen in order for the sins of people to be forgiven.

Turn to page 77 to read the real,
true *story of The Lord's Supper
from the Book of Matthew.*

A man named Saul was looking for Christians so he could put them in jail for being followers of Jesus.

While on his way to the city of Damascus, God struck Saul down with a bright light. God made Saul blind.

Not even blindness could stop Saul from his evil mission. He got a CHRISTIAN-SNIFFING-SEEING-EYE GOAT for himself and continued to find Christians and put them in jail.

Three days later, the Lord Jesus had a man named Ananias go to Saul and restore his sight. Saul proclaimed, "Jesus is the Son of God!" Later, Saul's name changed to Paul, and he became one of the most important people in the Bible as he shared the truth about Jesus throughout the world.

Turn to page 78 to read the real, true story of Saul's Conversion from the Book of Acts.

Paul went on to write many of the books of the New Testament that tell about how God changed his heart and about the truth of Jesus.

While we were God's enemies, God made friends with us through the death of His Son. Surely, now that we are God's friends, God will save us through His Son's life. And not only that, but now we are also very happy in God through our Lord Jesus Christ. Through Jesus we are now God's friends again.

Romans 5:10–11

Now, for the real, TRUE stories . . .

Creation

In the beginning, God created the sky and the earth. The earth was empty and had no form. Darkness covered the ocean, and God's Spirit was moving over the water.

Then God said, "Let there be light!" And there was light. He divided the light from the darkness. God named the light "day" and the darkness "night." Evening passed, and morning came. This was the first day.

Then God said, "Let there be something to divide the water in two!" So God made the air to divide the water in two. God named the air "sky." Evening passed, and morning came. This was the second day.

Then God said, "Let the water under the sky be gathered together so the dry land will appear." And it happened. God named the dry land "earth." Then God said, "Let the earth produce plants." And it happened. Evening passed, and morning came. This was the third day.

Then God said, "Let there be lights in the sky to separate day from night. They will be in the sky to give light to the earth." And it happened. Evening passed, and morning came. This was the fourth day.

Then God said, "Let the water be filled with living things. And let birds fly in the air above the earth." Evening passed, and morning came. This was the fifth day.

Then God said, "Let us make human beings in our image and likeness. And let them rule over the fish in the sea and the birds in the sky. Let them rule over the tame animals, over all the earth, and over all the small, crawling animals on the earth."

God looked at everything He had made, and it was very good. Evening passed, and morning came. This was the sixth day.

So the sky, the earth, and all that filled them were finished. By the seventh day, God finished the work He had been doing. So on the seventh day, He rested from all His work. God blessed the seventh day and made it a holy day. He made it holy because on that day He rested. He rested from all the work He had done in creating the world.

From the Book of Genesis, chapters 1 and 2.

Abraham and Sarah

God led Abraham outside. God said, "Look at the sky. There are so many stars you cannot count them. And your descendants will be too many to count."

Abraham believed the Lord. And the Lord accepted Abraham's faith, and that faith made him right with God.

God said to Abraham, "I will bless your wife Sarah. I will give her a son, and you will be the father. She will be the mother of many nations. Kings of nations will come from her."

Abraham bowed facedown on the ground and laughed. He said to himself, "Can a man have a child when he is one hundred years old? Can Sarah give birth to a child when she is ninety?"

Abraham and Sarah were very old. Sarah was past the age when women normally have children. So she laughed to herself, "My husband and I are too old to have a baby."

The Lord cared for Sarah as He had said. He did for her what He had promised. Sarah became pregnant. And she gave birth to a son for Abraham in his old age. Everything happened at the time God had said it would. Abraham named his son Isaac. Sarah gave birth to this son of Abraham.

Abraham was one hundred years old when his son Isaac was born. And Sarah said, "God has made me laugh. Everyone who hears about this will laugh with me. No one thought that I would be able to have Abraham's child. But I have given Abraham a son while he is old."

From the Book of Genesis, chapters 15, 17, 18, and 21

Joseph and His Brothers

Jacob lived in the land of Canaan. His son Joseph was a young man. He and his brothers cared for the flocks. Joseph was born when Jacob was old, so Jacob loved Joseph more than his other sons. He made Joseph a special robe. The brothers saw that their father loved Joseph more than he loved them. So they hated their brother.

Joseph had dreams that his brothers would bow down to him, and this angered his brothers even more, so they decided to trick him. While they were watching the sheep in the fields, Joseph came looking for them, and they threw him into an empty well. Some traders passed through the area, and the brothers sold Joseph to them as a slave.

The traders took Joseph to Egypt where they sold him to Potiphar, an officer to the king of Egypt. The Lord was with Joseph in everything he did, so Potiphar put Joseph in charge of everything. Joseph prospered and became very successful. He was named ruler of Egypt under the king.

Years later there was a terrible famine in Egypt, as Joseph had seen in a dream. He had wisely stored grain for such a time to keep the people alive. When his brothers went to Egypt to buy some grain, they didn't recognize their brother. But Joseph recognized them, and he gave them all that they needed and more. He forgave them for the bad things they had done to him, knowing that everything was in God's plan for good.

From the Book of Genesis, chapters 37–45

Manna in the Desert

The whole Israelite community came to the Desert of Sin. They came to this place on the fifteenth day of the second month after they had left Egypt. Then the whole Israelite community grumbled to Moses and Aaron in the desert. The Israelites said to them, "It would have been better if the Lord had killed us in the land of Egypt. There we had meat to eat. We had all the food we wanted. But you have brought us into this desert. You will starve us to death here."

The Lord said to Moses, "I will cause food to fall like rain from the sky. This food will be for all of you. Every day the people must go out and gather what they need for that day. I will do this to see if the people will do what I teach them. On the sixth day of each week, they are to gather twice as much as they gather on other days."

Then the Lord said to Moses, "I have heard the grumblings of the people of Israel. So tell them, 'At twilight you will eat meat. And every morning you will eat all the bread you want. Then you will know I am the Lord, your God.'"

That evening, quail came and covered the camp. And in the morning, dew lay around the camp. When the dew was gone, thin flakes like frost were on the desert ground. When the Israelites saw it, they asked each other, "What is that?" They asked this question because they did not know what it was.

The Israelites ate manna for forty years. They ate it until they came to the land where they settled. They ate manna until they came to the edge of the land of Canaan.

From the Book of Exodus, chapter 16.

The Ten Commandments

There was thunder and lightning with a thick cloud on the mountain. And there was a very loud blast from a trumpet. All the people in the camp were frightened. Then Moses led the people out of the camp to meet God. They stood at the foot of the mountain. Mount Sinai was covered with smoke. This happened because the Lord came down on it in fire. The smoke rose from the mountain like smoke from a furnace. And the whole mountain shook wildly. The sound from the trumpet became louder. Then Moses spoke, and the voice of God answered him.

So the Lord came down on the top of Mount Sinai. Then He called Moses to come up to the top of the mountain. So Moses went up. The Lord said to Moses, "Go down and warn the people. They must not force their way through to see me. If they do, many of them will die. Even the priests, who may come near me, must first prepare themselves. If they don't, I, the Lord, will punish them."

Moses told the Lord, "The people cannot come up Mount Sinai. You yourself told us to set a limit around the mountain. We made it holy."

The Lord said to him, "Go down and bring Aaron with you. But don't allow the priests or the people to force their way through. They must not come up to the Lord. If they do, I will punish them."

So Moses went down to the people and told them these things.

Then God spoke all these words:

"I am the Lord your God. I brought you out of the land of Egypt where you were slaves.

"You must not have any other gods except me.

"You must not make for yourselves any idols. Don't make something that looks like anything in the sky above or on the earth below or in the water below the land. You must not worship or serve any idol. This is because I, the Lord your God, am a jealous God. A person may sin against me and hate me. I will punish his children, even his grandchildren and great-grandchildren. But I will be very kind to thousands who love me and obey my commands.

1. Don't believe in other gods.
2. Don't love anything more than God.
3. Don't use God's name in a bad way.
4. Keep church-day Holy.
5. Love your Mother and Father.

6. Do not kill.
7. Be faithful to your spouse.
8. Do not steal.
9. Do not tell lies.
10. Don't want what other people have.

"You must not use the name of the Lord your God thoughtlessly. The Lord will punish anyone who is guilty and misuses His name.

"Remember to keep the Sabbath as a holy day. You may work and get everything done during six days each week. But the seventh day is a day of rest to honor the Lord your God. On that day no one may do any work: not you, your son or daughter, or your men or women slaves. Neither your animals nor the foreigners living in your cities may work. The reason is that in six days the Lord made everything. He made the sky, earth, sea, and everything in them. And on the seventh day, He rested. So the Lord blessed the Sabbath day and made it holy.

"Honor your father and your mother. Then you will live a long time in the land. The Lord your God is going to give you this land.

"You must not murder anyone.

"You must not be guilty of adultery.

"You must not steal.

"You must not tell lies about your neighbor in court.

"You must not want to take your neighbor's house. You must not want his wife or his men or women slaves. You must not want his ox or his donkey. You must not want to take anything that belongs to your neighbor."

The people heard the thunder and the trumpet. They saw the lightning on the mountain and smoke rising from the mountain. They shook with fear and stood far away from the mountain. Then they said to Moses, "Speak to us yourself. Then we will listen. But don't let God speak to us, or we will die."

Then Moses said to the people, "Don't be afraid. God has come to test you. He wants you to respect Him so you will not sin."

From the Book of Exodus, chapters 19 and 20.

Gideon

All the Midianites, the Amalekites, and other peoples from the east joined together. They came across the Jordan River and camped in the Valley of Jezreel. But the Spirit of the Lord entered Gideon! Gideon blew a trumpet to call the Abiezrites to follow him. He sent messengers to all of Manasseh. The people of Manasseh were called to follow Gideon. Gideon also sent messengers to the people of Asher, Zebulun, and Naphtali. They also went up to meet Gideon and his men.

Then Gideon said to God, "You said you would help me save Israel. I will put some wool on the threshing floor. Let there be dew only on the wool, but let all of the ground be dry. Then I will know what you said is true. I will know that you will use me to save Israel." And that is just what happened. Gideon got up early the next morning and squeezed the wool. He got a full bowl of water from the wool.

Then Gideon said to God, "Don't be angry with me. Let me ask just one more thing. Please let me make one more test. Let the wool be dry while the ground around it gets wet with dew." That night God did that very thing. Just the wool was dry, but the ground around it was wet with dew.

From the Book of Judges, chapter 6.

Mary and Baby Jesus

Jesus was born in the town of Bethlehem in Judea during the time when Herod was king. After Jesus was born, some wise men from the east came to Jerusalem. They asked, "Where is the baby who was born to be the King of the Jews? We saw His star in the east. We came to worship Him."

When King Herod heard about this new King of the Jews, he was troubled. And all the people in Jerusalem were worried, too. Herod called a meeting of all the leading priests and teachers of the law. He asked them where Christ would be born. They answered, "In the town of Bethlehem in Judea. The prophet wrote about this in the Scriptures:

'But you, Bethlehem, in the land of Judah,

you are important among the rulers of Judah. A ruler will come from you. He will be like a shepherd for my people, the Israelites.'"

Micah 5:2

Then Herod had a secret meeting with the wise men from the east. He learned from them the exact time they first saw the star. Then Herod sent the wise men to Bethlehem. He said to them, "Go and look carefully to find the child. When you find Him, come tell me. Then I can go worship Him, too."

The wise men heard the king and then left. They saw the same star they had seen in the east. It went before them until it stopped above the place where the child was. When the wise men saw the star, they were filled with joy. They went to the house where the child was and saw Him with His mother, Mary. They bowed down and worshiped the child. They opened the gifts they brought for Him. They gave Him treasures of gold, frankincense, and myrrh. But God warned the wise men in a dream not to go back to Herod. So they went home to their own country by a different way.

After they left, an angel of the Lord came to Joseph in a dream. The angel said, "Get up! Take the child and His mother and escape to Egypt. Herod will start looking for the child to kill Him. Stay in Egypt until I tell you to return."

So Joseph got up and left for Egypt during the night with the child and His mother. Joseph stayed in Egypt until Herod died. This was to make clear the full meaning of what the Lord had said through the prophet. The Lord said, "I called my Son out of Egypt."

From the Book of Matthew, chapter 2.

Young Jesus in the Temple

Joseph and Mary finished doing everything that the law of the Lord commanded. Then they went home to Nazareth, their own town in Galilee. The little child began to grow up. He became stronger and wiser, and God's blessings were with Him.

Every year Jesus' parents went to Jerusalem for the Passover Feast. When Jesus was twelve years old, they went to the feast as they always did. When the feast days were over, they went home. The boy Jesus stayed behind in Jerusalem, but His parents did not know it. Joseph and Mary traveled for a whole day. They thought that Jesus was with them in the group. Then they began to look for Him among their family and friends, but they did not find Him. So they went back to Jerusalem to look for Him there. After three days, they found Him. Jesus was sitting in the Temple with the religious teachers, listening to them and asking them questions. All who heard Him were amazed at His understanding and wise answers. When Jesus' parents saw Him, they were amazed. His mother said to Him, "Son, why did you do this to us? Your father and I were very worried about you. We have been looking for you."

Jesus asked, "Why did you have to look for me? You should have known that I must be where my Father's work is!" But they did not understand the meaning of what He said.

Jesus went with them to Nazareth and obeyed them. His mother was still thinking about all that had happened. Jesus continued to learn more and more and to grow physically. People liked Him, and He pleased God.

From the Book of Luke, chapter 2.

The Lord's Supper

On the first day of the Feast of Unleavened Bread, the followers came to Jesus. They said, "We will prepare everything for you to eat the Passover Feast. Where do you want to have the feast?"

Jesus answered, "Go into the city to a certain man. Tell him that the Teacher says, 'The chosen time is near. I will have the Passover Feast with my followers at your house.'" The followers did what Jesus told them to do, and they prepared the Passover Feast.

In the evening Jesus was sitting at the table with his followers. He said, "One of you will turn against me." This made the followers very sad. Each one said to Jesus, "Surely, Lord, I am not the one who will turn against you. Am I?"

Jesus answered, "The man who has dipped his hand with me into the bowl is the one who will turn against me. The Son of Man will die. The Scriptures say this will happen. But how terrible it will be for the person who gives the Son of Man to be killed. It would be better for him if he had never been born."

Then Judas said to Jesus, "Teacher, surely I am not the one. Am I?" (Judas was the one who would give Jesus to his enemies.)

Jesus answered, "Yes, it is you."

While they were eating, Jesus took some bread. He thanked God for it and broke it. Then He gave it to His followers and said, "Take this bread and eat it. This bread is my body."

Then Jesus took a cup. He thanked God for it and gave it to the followers. He said, "Every one of you drink this. This is my blood which begins the new agreement that God makes with His people. This blood is poured out for many to forgive their sins. I tell you this: I will not drink of this fruit of the vine again until that day when I drink it new with you in my Father's kingdom."

They sang a hymn. Then they went out to the Mount of Olives.

From the Book of Matthew, chapter 26.

Saul's Conversion

In Jerusalem, Saul was still trying to frighten the followers of the Lord by saying he would kill them. So he went to the high priest and asked him to write letters to the synagogues in the city of Damascus. Saul wanted the high priest to give him the authority to find people in Damascus who were followers of Christ's Way. If he found any there, men or women, he would arrest them and bring them back to Jerusalem.

So Saul went to Damascus. As he came near the city, a bright light from heaven suddenly flashed around him. Saul fell to the ground. He heard a voice saying to him, "Saul, Saul! Why are you doing things against me?"

Saul said, "Who are you, Lord?"

The voice answered, "I am Jesus. I am the One you are trying to hurt. Get up now and go into the city. Someone there will tell you what you must do."

The men traveling with Saul stood there, but they said nothing. They heard the voice, but they saw no one. Saul got up from the ground. He opened his eyes, but he could not see. So the men with Saul took his hand and led him into Damascus. For three days Saul could not see, and he did not eat or drink.

There was a follower of Jesus in Damascus named Ananias. The Lord spoke to Ananias in a vision, "Ananias!"

Ananias answered, "Here I am, Lord."

The Lord said to him, "Get up and go to the street called Straight Street. Find the house of Judas. Ask for a man named Saul from the city of Tarsus. He is there now, praying. Saul has seen a vision. In it a man named Ananias comes to him and lays his hands on him. Then he sees again."

But Ananias answered, "Lord, many people have told me about this man and the terrible things he did to your people in Jerusalem. Now he has come here to Damascus. The leading priests have given him the power to arrest everyone who worships you."

But the Lord said to Ananias, "Go! I have chosen Saul for an important work. He must tell about me to non-Jews, to kings, and to the people of Israel. I will show him how much he must suffer for my name."

So Ananias went to the house of Judas. He laid his hands on Saul and said, "Brother Saul, the Lord Jesus sent me. He is the one you saw on the road on your way here. He sent me so that you can see again and be filled with the Holy Spirit." Immediately, something that looked like fish scales fell from Saul's eyes. He was able to see again! Then Saul got up and was baptized. After eating some food, his strength returned.

From the Book of Acts, chapter 9.